CAKES

English Favourites

A selection of the best

British recipes

Diana Baker

Copyright © 2016 Diana Baker

Copyright © 2016 Editorial Imagen.
Córdoba, Argentina

Editorialimagen.com
All rights reserved.

Corrected and Revised Edition, July 2016

All rights reserved. No part of this book may be reproduced by any means (including electronic, mechanical or otherwise, such as photocopying, recording or any storage or reproduction of information) without written permission of the author, except for brief portions quoted for review purposes.

CATEGORY: Recipes

Printed in the United States of America

ISBN-13:
ISBN-10:

Content

Introduction 1

Hints to ensure success 3

To prove the temperature of the oven 5

Weights and Measures 7

Recipes for Cakes 9

    Key Recipe for a Small Cake 11
    Angel Cake 12
    Chocolate Angel Cake 12
    Apricot Cake 13
    Bachelor Cake 14
    Banana Cake 15
    Birthday Cake 16
    Bittersweet Nougat Cake 17
    Black Currant Cake 19
    Bride's Delight Cake 20
    Buttermilk Cake – (no eggs) 21
    Caramel Layer Cake 22
    Cherry Cake 24
    Chestnut Cake 25
    Chocolate Cake – I 26
    Chocolate Cake – II 28
    Chocolate Cake – III 29
    Chocolate Cake – IV 30
    Chocolate Roll 31
    Poor Man's Chocolate Cake 32
    Coconut Cream Sandwich 33

Cornflour Cake	35
Devil's Food Cake	36
Economy Cake	38
Faecula Roll	39
Fresh Fruit Refrigerator Cake	40
Economy Fruit Cake	41
Fruit Cake – I	43
Fruit Cake – II	44
Fruit Cake – III	45
Milkless and Eggless Fruit Cake	46
Genoa Cake	47
Gingerbread Banana Shortcake	48
Maryland Gingerbread	49
Sour Cream Gingerbread	50
Spiced Gingerbread 'Splendid'	51
Sponge Gingerbread - (no eggs)	52
Hungarian Rhapsody	53
Lancashire Dainty	55
Lazy-Daisy Cake	56
Light Layer Cake	58
Madeira Cake	59
Mahogany Cake	60
Maple Nut Cake	62
Mocha Sponge Cake - (no cooking required)	63
Multicoloured Cake	64
Nut-loaf Cake	65
Nut Sponge Cake	66
One Egg Cake	67
Orange Cake	68
Orange Sponge Cake	69
Perfect Yellow Cake	71
Pineapple Upside Down Cake	73

Plain Cake 74
Raisin Cake 75
Red Devil Cake 76
Jam Sandwich Roll 77
Scotch Cake 78
Belgian Shortbread 79
Canadian Shortbread 80
Scotch Shortbread 81
Shortbread 82
Soda Cake 83
Sponge Cake – I 84
Sponge Cake – II 85
Favourite Sponge Cake 86
Sultana Cake 87
Sunshine Cake of Yellow Maize 88
Swiss Roll 89
Vinegar Cake – I 90
Vinegar Cake – II 91
Walnut Cake – I 92
Walnut Cake – II 93
Walnut Surprise Cake 94
Small Wedding Cake 96
Whipped Cream Cake 99

Icing 101

American Icing 103
Never-Fail Chocolate Frosting 104
Coffee Icing 105
Never-Fail Icing - Ready in 4 minutes 106
Nut Filling and Icing 107
Sea-Breeze Frosting 108
White Icing - (hard icing) 109

Fillings 111

    Delicious Chocolate Filling 113
    Filling for Leftover Egg Yolks 115
    Lemon Cheese Filling 116
    Synthetic Cream 117

More Books of Interest 119

Spanish Related Books 121

Introduction

Welcome to this recipe book for cakes with a British flavour. These are many of the typical favourites for the once traditional five o' clock tea including chocolate cakes, fruit cakes, gingerbreads and shortbreads. You will also find a variety of icings and fillings to give your cakes an alternative decoration and/or flavour.

There are never-ending reasons to bake a delicious cake – be it just for the family's sake or for a get together with friends or because you want to entertain your loved ones on a special occasion of the year such as at Christmas or a birthday...or simply because you fancy something good and sweet.

The following recipes are quick and easy to prepare and with accessible and uncomplicated ingredients.

I'm sure you'll discover that many recipes will become long-time favorites in your home.

Let's begin with some helpful tips to ensure that nothing goes wrong.

Hints to ensure success

- Always read the recipe through carefully and understand it before starting. Then collect together and prepare all the ingredients to be used.

- Always sift the flour.

- Always stir in the same direction.

- Grease all cake tins except when making angel and sponge cakes.

- Never bang the oven door.

- Always work neatly; use as few utensils as possible, and clear up as the cooking proceeds.

- Never mix new flour with old.

- Never begrudge the time you spend on good mixing.

Cakes are often spoiled by over beating after the baking powder has been added; it is therefore advisable to add the baking powder, sifted with a small quantity of the flour, last. One's usual experience is that if you take no care and make a hurried cake for the family, it is lighter than the cake made for the special occasion.

The reason is probably because too much beating has been done after baking powder has been added, or that too much flour has been used.

To prove the temperature of the oven

A simple and effective method of proving the heat of the oven when no thermometer is available:

Heat the oven for 10 minutes, then, put a piece of white paper in the centre of the oven. The temperature of the oven will be correct if the paper becomes brown in the time specified below:

Oven	Degrees	Paper
Very hot	446ºF–500ºF	½ minute
Hot	392ºF-428ºF	1 minute
Moderate	338ºF-374ºF	1 ½ minutes
Slow	320ºF	2 minutes

Electric and Gas equivalents

275°F = 140°C or Gas Mark 1
300°F = 150°C or Gas Mark 2
325°F = 165°C or Gas Mark 3
350°F = 180°C or Gas Mark 4
375°F = 190°C or Gas Mark 5
400°F = 200°C or Gas Mark 6
425°F = 220°C or Gas Mark 7
450°F = 230°C or Gas Mark 8

Weights and Measures

All containers used for measuring should be filled level, unless otherwise stated in the recipe, smoothing off any surplus with a knife. When a cup in indicated, a cup holding ½ pint should be used.

1 Teaspoon equals 5 g or 60 drops

1 Dessertspoon equals 10 g or 2 teaspoons

1 Tablespoon equals 15 g or 3 teaspoons

1 wine glass equals 100 g or 4 tablespoons

1 cup equals ½ pint or ¼ litre or 16 tablespoons

1 lb. equals 16 ounces or 460 g

½ lb. equals 8 ounces or 230 g

1 ounce equals 28 ½ g

3 ½ cups flours are equivalent to .... 480 g or 1 lb.

2 cups granulated sugar .... 400 g or 14 ozs

2 ½ cups icing sugar............................... 300 g or 11 ozs

2 1/4 cups brown sugar........................... 500 g or l lb.

1 cup seedless raisins .... 200 g or 7 ozs

1 cup currants etc. .... 200 g or 7 ozs

2 cups chopped nuts .... 240 g or ½ lb.

1 cup butter or lard .... 230 g or ½ lb.

Recipes for Cakes

Key Recipe for a Small Cake

6 tablespoons flour
4 tablespoons sugar
4 tablespoons butter
2 eggs
2 heaped teaspoons baking powder
2 tablespoon milk
A pinch of salt

Add any flavouring desired, such as grated chocolate, grated orange rind, caraway seeds, or whatever you fancy.

Angel Cake

8 egg whites
¾ cup sugar
¾ cup flour
1 teaspoon baking powder
½ teaspoon cream of tartar
¼ teaspoon salt
A little essence, vanilla or almond

Beat whites to a very firm, stiff froth.

Add cream of tartar, beat well.

Lightly fold in sugar, next, add the flour sifted 3 times with the salt and baking powder.

Add flavouring.

Bake in a moderate oven (350° F) in ungreased tube tin for about 45 minutes.

Remove from oven and invert the cake in tin.

Turn out when cold.

Chocolate Angel Cake

Proceed as in previous recipe.

Sift a little cocoa with the flour.

Apricot Cake

½ cup dried apricot
1 egg
¾ cup sugar
2 tablespoons melted butter
2 cups sifted butter
3 teaspoons baking powder
¼ teaspoon bicarbonate of soda
A pinch of salt
Approximately ¾ cup milk
¾ cup chopped nuts

Soak apricots in water from 30 to 45 minutes. Drain and pass through coarse mincer.

Beat egg well with sugar.

Add butter, flour, baking powder, bicarbonate of soda, salt and milk.

Lastly, add apricots and nuts.

Bake in greased tin for about 1 hour.

Bachelor Cake

16 heaped tablespoons flour
10 heaped tablespoons sultanas
8 tablespoons sugar
4 tablespoons butter
2 eggs
1 teaspoons bicarbonate of soda
½ teacup almonds or walnuts
½ teacup candied peel
2 tablespoons treacle (golden syrup)
1 teacup milk

Rub butter into flour, and add dry ingredients, then the eggs and treacle.

Warm the milk and dissolve bicarbonate of soda in it and add to mixture.

Keep back part of the chopped nuts to sprinkle on top of cake when putting into oven.

Cook in a very slow oven, for about 1 hour, or more.

Banana Cake

3 mashed bananas
4 ozs butter
1 teacup flour
1 teacup sugar
1 egg
½ teaspoon salt
½ teaspoon bicarbonate of soda

Cream butter.

Add sugar slowly, beating in well, then the egg, salt, bananas, flour and bicarbonate.

Bake for 45 minutes in a moderate oven.

Birthday Cake

3½ cups flour
1 ½ butter
1 cup sugar
1½ cups sultanas
2 ½ cups currants
2 tablespoons glacé cherries
½ cup candied peel
4 eggs
Milk to mix

Wash and dry well the currants and sultanas.

Cut the cherries and peel into small pieces.

Sift the flour well.

Grease and line a large round cake tin with buttered paper.

Cream the butter and sugar together. Beat the eggs separately into the creamed butter and sugar, and beat well for 15 minutes.

Mix all the fruit with the flour, adding gradually, and mixing all thoroughly together.

Place in tin and bake in a moderately hot oven for about 4 hours.

Bittersweet Nougat Cake

2/3 butter
1 teaspoon salt
1 teaspoon vanilla
1½ cups sugar
2 whole eggs and 2 egg yolks
3 tablespoons melted chocolate
1 teaspoon baking powder
¾ teaspoon bicarbonate of soda
2 ¼ cups sifted flour
1 cup milk

Cream the butter.

Add sugar gradually, then the salt and vanilla. Beat until light and fluffy.

Add the beaten eggs and mix thoroughly.

Then add the melted chocolate and blend well.

Sift the flour, baking powder and bicarbonate of soda together 3 times, and add gradually and alternately to cream mixture, with the milk, mixing after each addition.

Pour into two deep 9-inch layer pans, previously greased or buttered.

Bake in moderate oven for 30 to 35 minutes.

Nougat Frosting:

2 egg whites, unbeaten
1½ cups granulated sugar
4 tablespoons water
2 tablespoons golden syrup
2 tablespoons honey
¼ teaspoon cream of tartar
½ teaspoon vanilla
¼ cup blanched chopped almonds

Put egg whites, sugar, water, syrup, honey and cream of tartar in top of double boiler, and mix well.

Place over rapidly boiling water and beat constantly with egg beater until mixture will hold a peak (about 7 minutes).

Remove from fire; add vanilla and beat until thick enough to spread.

Add the almonds to 1/3 of the frosting and spread between the layers.

Spread plain frosting on top and sides of cake.

Black Currant Cake

1/3 cup butter
1 cup sugar
2 eggs
2 cups flour
3 teaspoons baking powder
½ teaspoon salt
¼ teaspoon cinnamon
¼ teaspoon nutmeg
1/8 teaspoon cloves
1/8 teaspoon spice
2/3 cup milk
½ cup black currant jam
½ cup chopped walnuts

Cream butter and sugar.

Add eggs one by one and beat well.

Sift flour with dry ingredients; add to mixture with the milk.

Stir until all the ingredients are well mixed.

Put in greased square baking tin and bake for 1 hour.

Bride's Delight Cake

1 cup milk
1 ½ cups sugar
3½ teaspoons baking powder
2 cups currants
2 cups raisins
4 cups flour
1 cup butter
1 teaspoon mixed spice
4 yolks and 4 whites beaten separately
Vanilla essence

Cream butter and sugar.

Add the beaten yolks and milk, then the dry ingredients (which have been previously well mixed).

Mix in lastly the whites well beaten.

Line a cake tin (any kind) with greaseproof paper, and pour mixture in.

Bake in a moderate oven for about 1 ¼ hours.

Buttermilk Cake – (no eggs)

½ cup butter (4 ozs)
1 cup brown sugar
A little syrup
1 cup buttermilk (soured is best)
2 cups flour
½ teaspoon nutmeg
½ teaspoon cinnamon
½ tablespoon mixed spice (or a little less)
1 heaped teaspoon bicarbonate of soda
1 cup fruit and peel
A pinch of salt

Cream the butter and sugar.

Warm the syrup.

Dissolve the bicarbonate of soda in milk.

Add the well sifted dry ingredients and fruit and mix well.

Bake in a moderate oven from about 45 minutes to 1 hour.

Caramel Layer Cake

½ cup shortening
1 cup sugar
1¾ cups flour
3 teaspoons baking powder
3 egg whites
1 teaspoon vanilla essence
¼ teaspoon salt
2/3 cup milk

Cream butter.

Add sugar slowly, beating in well.

Add unbeaten egg whites, one at a time, beating well after each addition.

Add flavouring.

Sift together flour, baking powder and salt.

Add alternately with milk to first mixture.

Put into well-greased, medium sized tin.

Bake for 50 minutes.

Caramel Icing:

2 cups brown sugar
1 cup milk or cream
1 tablespoon butter
A few drops vanilla

Mix ingredients and boil, without stirring until a soft ball can be formed.

Add vanilla and beat until creamy.

Cherry Cake

2 eggs
The weight of 3 eggs in sugar
The weight of 3 eggs in butter
The weight of 4 eggs in flour
½ cup glacé cherries
1 small teaspoon baking powder

Beat the butter and sugar to a cream.

Then add the eggs well beaten, next the flour, then the cherries cut into slices, and lastly the baking powder.

Beat all together.

Butter and flour a tin; put the mixture in and bake in a moderate oven for 25 to 30 minutes.

Chestnut Cake

1 lb. chestnuts
1 cup sugar
4 eggs
Vanilla
Whipped cream

Remove outside skin of chestnuts and put them in a hot oven to remove also the inside skin.

Cook with a little sugar and a small piece of vanilla till soft enough to put through a sieve or press, and let cool.

Beat sugar well with egg yolks; add gradually the cooled chestnuts and the beaten whites of the eggs.

Cook for 25 to 30 minutes in a moderate oven.

Before serving, cover with whipped cream.

Chocolate Cake – I

½ cup butter
1¾ flour
1 ½ sugar
3 eggs
½ cup milk
3 bars chocolate
2 teaspoons baking powder
½ teaspoon vanilla essence

Beat butter and half of the sugar together.

Beat the yolks with the other half of the sugar and add to the first mixture.

Add the chocolate, then the flour sifted with the baking powder.

Then add the milk and essence, and lastly the well beaten whites of egg.

Place in buttered baking tin and cook for about 20 minutes.

When cold cover with the following icing:

Icing:

1½ cups butter
½ cup water
1 cup sugar
4 yolks

4 bars chocolate

First boil the sugar and water together until a syrup is formed.

Then pour this into the already beaten up yolks, beating until frothy.

Add to this the butter and lastly the melted chocolate.

Chocolate Cake – II

1 egg
3 heaped tablespoons dark cocoa
½ teacup butter
1 teacup milk
1 teacup castor sugar
1 teaspoon bicarbonate of soda
1½ teacups flour
1 teaspoon vanilla

Beat egg, add cocoa and ½ teacup milk and cook until thick, stirring constantly and remove from fire to cool.

Cream the butter and sugar.

Add ½ teacup milk.

Sift bicarbonate with flour and add to creamed butter and sugar.

Then stir vanilla into the mixture and add the cocoa mixture (which need not be very cool) and beat all together thoroughly.

Bake in moderate oven.

Ice if you like.

Chocolate Cake – III

3 tablespoons cocoa
1 cup sugar
1 cup flour
1 teaspoon cream of tartar
½ teaspoon bicarbonate of soda
2 eggs
¼ butter
Milk
A pinch of salt

Sift dry ingredients together.

Melt the butter, break the eggs into it and fill the cup with milk.

Stir into dry ingredients and beat well.

Bake in a moderate oven from 40 to 45 minutes.

Chocolate Cake – IV

4½ tablespoons butter (4½ ozs)
1 teacup fine sugar
1½ teacups flour
3 tablespoons cocoa
3 eggs
½ cup milk
2 teaspoons baking powder
A pinch of salt

Cream the butter and sugar.

Add the egg yolks and beat well.

Sift together the flour, cocoa, and salt and add alternately with the milk until all is used up.

Then add the baking powder, and lastly the stiffly beaten egg whites.

Bake for about 1 hour.

Chocolate Roll

5 eggs
½ cup sugar
2 tablespoons flour
3 tablespoons cocoa

Separate eggs, beat yolks until light.

Add sugar and beat again.

Add flour and cocoa, and beat well. Lastly fold in stiffly beaten egg whites.

Put into a flat tin and bake for 10 minutes in hot oven.

Sprinkle with granulated sugar.

Roll and let stand until cold then cover with the following icing:

Icing:

2 squares chocolate
2 tablespoons butter
Icing sugar
Approximately 1 tablespoon milk

Melt chocolate, milk and butter over stove.

When melted, remove from fire and add sufficient icing sugar to make the right consistency to spread.

Poor Man's Chocolate Cake

3 tablespoons butter
1 cup sugar
1½ cups flour
1 cup sour milk
1 teaspoon baking soda
1/2 cup cocoa
1 teaspoon vanilla essence
A pinch of salt

Cream the butter.

Sift the dry ingredients together 4 times.

Add vanilla essence.

Mix well.

Bake in moderate oven.

Coconut Cream Sandwich

2 tablespoons coconut
1 cup flour
1 teaspoon baking powder
1 egg and 1 yolk
3 tablespoons sugar
1 tablespoon butter
Milk to mix

Sift the flour and baking powder, and add the coconut.

Whisk the eggs and sugar until thick and creamy.

Warm the butter enough to melt.

Gradually stir the flour and coconut into the egg and sugar with the melted butter.

Add the milk as required.

Mix all together lightly and bake in a hot oven from 10 to 15 minutes.

When cold cut in half, spread with the following filling:

Filling:

4 tablespoons icing sugar
2 tablespoons butter

1 tablespoon coconut
Vanilla essence

Beat the butter and sugar.

Add the coconut and a few drops of essence, and mix together.

Spread jam on top of the cake and sprinkle with coconut.

Cornflour Cake

½ cup butter
1 cup sugar
3 egg whites
1 cup flour
¾ cup cornflour
1 heaped teaspoon baking powder
½ cup sweet milk
1 teaspoon flavouring extract

Cream sugar and butter.

Add the milk.

Stir in the cornflour, flour, baking powder and a pinch of salt and mix well together.

Then add flavouring extract and lastly the whites of egg beaten very stiff.

Bake in a loaf-shaped tin.

Devil's Food Cake

1 cup brown sugar
1 cup grated chocolate
½ cup sweet milk
Pinch of salt

Bring these ingredients slowly to the boil and when cool pour into the following mixture:

1 cup brown sugar
½ cup butter
1/3 milk
3 egg yolks well beaten
2 cups flour
2 teaspoons baking powder
2 egg whites, beaten

Cream the sugar and butter.

Add milk and egg yolks, flour, baking powder and lastly the beaten egg whites.

Bake in a slow oven.

Ice with white icing or fill with cream.

White Icing:

4 cups icing sugar
1 egg white
A little lemon juice or almond essence

Mix all the ingredients together until smooth and spread with a knife warmed in hot water.

Economy Cake

2 cups flour
2 teaspoons baking powder
¼ teaspoon salt
4 tablespoons butter
1 cup sugar
1 egg
¾ cup milk
1 teaspoon vanilla

Cream butter.

Add sugar and well-beaten egg.

Then add the flour and milk little by little, with the vanilla, salt and baking powder.

Put in a ring shaped baking tin and bake for 25 to 30 minutes.

Faecula Roll

3 eggs (beat yolks and whites separately)
3 tablespoons sugar
3 tablespoons potato flour
1 scant tablespoon baking powder

Mix all together.

Add the stiffly beaten egg whites last.

Spread on a large baking sheet.

Bake in a moderate oven.

Fresh Fruit Refrigerator Cake

1 1/3 cups (1 tin) condensed milk
¼ lemon juice
1 cup quartered cherries, whole raspberries or sliced strawberries
24 vanilla wafers

Blend together the condensed milk and lemon juice.

Add prepared fruit.

Line narrow, oblong tin or a springform cake tin, with wax paper. Cover with fruit mixture.

Add layer of wafers, alternating in this way until fruit mixture is used; finishing with layer of wafers.

Chill in refrigerator for 6 hours or longer.

To serve, turn out on small platter and carefully remove wax paper.

Top may be decorated with fruit. Cut in slices and serve plain or with whipped cream.

Economy Fruit Cake

1 cup sugar
2½ cups flour
3 teaspoons baking powder
¼ teaspoon bicarbonate of soda
½ teaspoon ground cloves
1 teaspoon cinnamon
1 cinnamon nutmeg
½ teaspoon salt
4 tablespoons finely cut citron
½ cup seedless raisins
½ cup currants
1 cup melted butter or lard
½ chopped walnuts
4 eggs
A few drops vanilla essence

Sift flour, salt and baking powder.

Add the remaining dry ingredients, mixing well.

Now stir in thoroughly the raisins finely chopped, currants, citron, and nuts.

Whip eggs and sugar till light and creamy.

Add cool melted shortening, also flavouring to taste and beat well.

Add to this the sifted dry ingredients, mixing well, adding a little milk to bring it to the right consistency. Mixture should drop easily off spoon.

Place in a well-greased baking tin and bake in a moderate oven for 1 ¼ hours.

Makes an 8-inch cake.

Fruit Cake – I

4 teaspoons flour
2 teacups butter
2 teacups sugar
1 teaspoon baking powder
8 eggs
2 teacups currants
2 teacups sultanas
2 teacups raisins
1 teacup candied peel
Grated rind of 1 lemon
2 tablespoons brandy
A little nutmeg
2 teacup almonds

Cream butter and sugar.

Add eggs and flour alternately until it is all worked in, then add the rest of the ingredients.

Beat up well and bake in a buttered tin.

Cook from 2 ½ to 3 hours in a hot oven to start with, afterwards lowering the temperature.

Fruit Cake – II

4 teacups flour
2 teacups sugar
1 teacup butter (7ozs)
5 eggs
¾ cup milk
2 teacups each of raisins and currants
1 teacup sultanas
½ cup chopped walnuts
A pinch salt
2 teaspoons cream of tartar
1 teaspoon bicarbonate of soda
Essence according to taste

Cream butter and sugar.

Add the beaten eggs and milk, then the dry ingredients (which have been previously well mixed).

Line a cake tin (any kind) with greaseproof paper, and pour mixture in.

Bake in a moderate oven for about 1 ¼ hours.

Fruit Cake – III

*4 cups flour
2 cups butter
2 cups sugar
8 eggs
1 teaspoon baking powder
6 cups fruit
Pinch of salt and nutmeg*

Cream the butter and sugar.

Beat the eggs and add to the mixture.

Sift the flour, salt and nutmeg together and then add the baking powder, and lastly the fruit.

Bake for 2 hours.

Milkless and Eggless Fruit Cake

Put the following ingredients into a saucepan and boil for three minutes:

1 cup brown sugar
2 cups seedless raisins
1 cup water
1/3 cup butter
¼ teaspoon grated nutmeg
1 teaspoon cinnamon
½ teaspoon ground cloves
Pinch of salt

Let cool and then add:

1 teaspoon baking soda dissolved in a little hot water
2 cups flour sifted with
½ teaspoon baking powder

Bake in a loaf shape tin for 1 hour at 350° F.

This cake improves with time like a good fruit cake.

Genoa Cake

1 cup butter
1 cup sugar
2 cups currants (or sultanas or ½ of each)
2 ½ cups flour
1 ½ teaspoons baking soda
1 teaspoon ginger
½ teaspoon mixed spice
A pinch of salt
1 cup hot water

Cream butter and sugar.

Add egg and syrup, then dry ingredients which have been sifted together.

Add hot water last and beat until smooth.

The mixture is soft but it makes a fine cake.

Bake in greased shallow pan 35 to 40 minutes in a moderate oven.

Gingerbread Banana Shortcake

1 ¾ flour
1 teaspoon baking powder
1 teaspoon ground ginger
½ teaspoon cinnamon
½ teaspoon salt
½ teaspoon bicarbonate of soda
3 tablespoons butter
½ cup sugar
1 egg
½ cup golden syrup or molasses
½ boiling water

Sift together all the dry ingredients.

Cream butter, add sugar gradually, then the beaten egg and golden syrup.

Add the dry ingredients, and mix thoroughly.

Lastly add boiling water.

Beat well and pour into 2 greased layer cake tins.

Bake in moderate oven 350° F from 20 to 30 minutes.

While slightly warm put sweetened whipped cream and sliced bananas between layers an on top.

Maryland Gingerbread

¾ cup melted butter
¾ cup brown sugar
2ggs
2 ¼ cups flour
2 ½ teaspoons baking powder
¾ teaspoon baking soda
¾ cup molasses
2 teaspoons ginger
1 ½ teaspoons cinnamon
½ teaspoon ground cloves
½ teaspoon grated nutmeg
1 cup boiling water

Add beaten eggs to sugar, molasses and melted butter.

Then add flour sifted with other dry ingredients.

Add boiling water last.

Bake in greased shallow pan in moderate oven at 350° F for 40 minutes.

Serve hot or cold.

Sour Cream Gingerbread

1 cup brown sugar
2 eggs
2 cups flour
1 teaspoon bicarbonate of soda
1 teaspoon salt
1 tablespoon ginger
½ teaspoon each of cinnamon and cloves
1 cup sour cream
½ molasses

Mix all dry ingredients.

Then add all moist ingredients, which should be well mixed previously.

Bake in moderate oven for about 20 minutes.

Spiced Gingerbread 'Splendid'

1 teacup butter
1 teacup sugar
3 eggs
3 heaped cups flour
1 teaspoon baking powder
1 teaspoon bicarbonate of soda
1 cup sour milk
1 chopped raisins
1 teaspoon ginger
1 teaspoon cinnamon
1 teaspoon mixed spice
1 nutmeg
1 cup treacle or some brown sugar

Warm the treacle.

Mix with the milk and add to the sugar and butter, creamed.

Add the beaten yolks and the whites whipped stiff, then the flour, in which the other ingredients have been well mixed.

Bake in a shallow greased tin, in a moderate oven.

Sponge Gingerbread - (no eggs)

½ cup butter (4 ozs)
1¼ teacups castor sugar
½ teacup golden syrup
1 teacup milk
1 heaped teaspoon bicarbonate of soda
1 dessertspoon spice
2 dessertspoons ground ginger
A pinch of salt
2 cups flour

(Sultanas or raisins may be added if preferred).

Cream butter and sugar.

Warm the syrup.

Dissolve the bicarbonate of soda in the milk and mix.

Bake in a shallow tin in a moderate oven for about ½ to ¾ hour.

Hungarian Rhapsody

10 eggs
450 g sugar
300 g ground nuts
3 teaspoons breadcrumbs
230 g chocolate
200 g butter
A little baking powder
A pinch of salt
Almonds to decorate cake

Cake mixture:

Beat the whites to a very stiff froth with the salt.

When firm add the ground nuts, 300 g of the sugar, the baking powder and breadcrumbs, and fold lightly together.

Divide the mixture into three portions.

Place the first portion onto a well buttered baking dish and cook for about 20 minutes; remove from oven when well browned.

Repeat the same process with each of the layers.

The cream:

Mix well the remaining amount of the sugar with the yolks.

Cook in double saucepan until it loses its raw flavour.

Add the melted chocolate a little at a time, stirring continually until it is completely cold.

Then add the creamed butter.

Spread between the layers and over all the cake.

Mark in squares and put an almond in the centre of each square.

Lancashire Dainty

1¾ cups flour
3 tablespoons butter
1 teaspoon bicarbonate of soda
4 tablespoons sugar
1 egg
1 teacup milk (sour if possible)
Currants or vanilla essence

Mix flour with butter.

Add bicarbonate of soda and sugar and mix well.

Add the egg, well beaten and milk, then the currants or vanilla for flavouring.

Bake in greased oblong tin in moderate oven.

This mixture may also be baked in 2 baking tins and served with a layer of jam in the centre.

Sprinkle sugar on the top.

Lazy-Daisy Cake

2 eggs
1 cup sugar
1 cup sifted flour
1 teaspoon baking powder
¼ teaspoon
1 teaspoon vanilla
½ cup milk
1 tablespoon butter

Beat eggs then add the sugar, flour, baking powder and salt.

Then add vanilla.

Lastly, heat milk plus butter and add.

Bake in 8 x 10 inch pan for about 20 minutes in moderate oven.

Cover with the following sauce:

Sauce:

10 tablespoons brown sugar
4 tablespoon butter
4 tablespoons milk
½ cup grated coconut or nuts

Cook together the sugar, butter and milk for about 5 minutes.

Add coconut or nuts.

Pour over cake (still in the pan, after it has finished baking) and put under the broiler and brown on the top.

Watch carefully as coconut burns easily.

Light Layer Cake

2 cups flour
1 ¼ cups sugar
½ cup butter
4 small teaspoons baking powder
2 eggs
1 teaspoon lemon essence
1 teaspoon vanilla essence
½ cup milk

Beat sugar and butter to cream.

Beat in egg yolks.

Add the flour and milk alternately.

Add the essence, the well beaten whites and the baking powder.

Bake in two sandwich tins in a fairly hot oven for about 20 minutes.

Madeira Cake

Whisk 4 eggs and add by slow degrees in the following order:

*5 tablespoons sifted sugar
1 1/3 cups flour
1 teaspoon baking powder
4 tablespoons butter, just melted
Grated rind of 1 lemon*

Bake for 1 hour in a moderate oven.

Mahogany Cake

½ cup butter
½ cups sugar
3 eggs
2 cups fine flour
1 teaspoon vanilla essence
¼ teaspoon baking soda
2½ teaspoons baking powder
2/3 cup milk
½ cup cocoa
½ cup milk

Cook cocoa and milk together until smooth and thick, cool.

Cream butter.

Add sugar slowly, beating in well.

Add unbeaten eggs, one at a time, beating well after each addition.

Add flavouring.

Sift together dry ingredients; add alternately with milk to creamed mixture.

Add chocolate mixture and mix well.

Bake in 3 greased 9-inch layer cake tins in moderate oven at 350° F about 20 minutes or bake in oblong baking tin for about 30 minutes.

Put layers together and cover top and sides of cake with frosting.

Cut into squares to serve.

Frosting:

1 cup butter
1 cup icing sugar
2 egg yolks
1 teaspoon vanilla extract

Cream butter.

Add sugar slowly, beating in well.

When very creamy and a light colour, add the yolks one at a time, beating well after each addition and constantly.

Add flavouring.

This cream must be kept in a cool place (if summer, in the refrigerator) until ready for use.

This cream may be also made without the egg yolks.

Maple Nut Cake

½ cup butter
1 cup brown sugar
2 eggs
1½ cups flour
2 tablespoons baking powder
½ cup milk
¼ teaspoon salt
1 teaspoon vanilla essence
1 cup chopped walnuts

Cream butter and sugar.

Add the well-whisked yolks of eggs; beat well.

Add half the milk and flour; beat well.

Add remainder of milk and flour, beat again.

Add baking powder, essence and nuts.

When all is well mixed add the well-whisked whites of egg, to which has been added the salt.

Cook 35 to 45 minutes in buttered cake tin.

Mocha Sponge Cake - (no cooking required)

1 cup butter
5 egg yolks
4 tablespoons sugar
24 sponge fingers
A little strong coffee (very concentrated)
A little rum
Some almonds or peanuts to decorate

Cream the butter and sugar.

Add the yolks gradually, beating well and lastly the coffee.

Dip the sponge fingers in rum.

Place 4 sponge fingers on a plate, spread them well with the cream.

Place the next four horizontally across the others, again spreading with the cream and so on until none remain.

Press between two plates with a weight on top, and leave for a short time.

Then cover the whole cake with the cream and spread a few almonds or peanuts over it all.

Multicoloured Cake

The weight of 3 eggs in butter, castor sugar and flour

3 eggs
½ teaspoon baking powder
3 dessertspoons milk
Jam

Beat butter to a cream. Add yolks of eggs.

Sift the baking powder with the flour. Stir in the flour and sugar, mix well all together; add the milk.

Beat egg whites to a stiff froth, and stir them well into the mixture.

Divide into three. Leave one plain, colour one pink and one chocolate.

Put in sandwich tins and bake 20 minutes in moderate oven.

When cold, cut into fingers and spread each layer with jam, leaving the top layer free. (Arrange colours alternately).

Icing:

1 cup icing sugar, rolled and sifted and made into a smooth paste with the juice of an orange.

Nut-loaf Cake

2 teacups butter
2 teacups sugar
4 egg yolks
4 egg whites
4 teacups flour
5 teaspoons baking powder
A little milk
2 teacups chopped nuts
Grated rind of 1 lemon or vanilla essence

Beat butter and sugar together and add egg yolks one by one, beating well.

Add milk, a little at a time.

Mix in lemon rind and the flour, beating well all the time.

Add stiffly beaten whites, and lastly the chopped nuts.

Bake in long buttered baking tin in a moderate oven, 350° F.

Cover with any desired icing.

Nut Sponge Cake

7 tablespoons sugar
7 eggs
6 tablespoons flour
1 teaspoon baking powder

Beat whites to stiff froth.

Add the sugar and beat again.

Next add yolks, sifted flour and baking powder.

Bake in fairly hot oven in ungreased pan.

Invert cake in pan, and let stand until cold.

Nut Filling:

1 large cup walnuts
2 tablespoons butter
2 tablespoons rum or brandy
3 egg yolks
1 teacup milk
1 teacup sugar

Mix all well together and stir over slow fire until it thickens; do not allow to boil.

One Egg Cake

4 tablespoons butter
1 cup sugar
1 egg, unbeaten
2 cups flour
2 teaspoons baking powder
¼ teaspoon slat
¾ cup milk
1 teaspoon vanilla

Sift the flour two or three times with the salt and baking powder.

Cream butter and sugar gradually beating until light and fluffy.

Add the egg and beat well.

Add flour and milk alternately mixing well after each addition.

Add vanilla.

Bake in a moderate oven for about 25 minutes.

Orange Cake

4 tablespoons butter (4 ozs)
3 tablespoons sugar
3 eggs
5 tablespoons flour
1 teaspoon baking powder
1 orange

Beat butter and sugar to a cream.

Add eggs separately, then the flour and a little grated orange peel and juice.

Bake for about ½ hour in rather quick oven.

Mix a little orange juice with icing sugar and a little rind and spread on top.

When set, decorate with crystallized orange jelly sweets.

Orange Sponge Cake

3 egg whites
1 teaspoon cream of tartar
3 egg yolks 1 cup sugar
1¼ cups flour
2 teaspoons grated orange rind
1 ½ teaspoons baking powder
1/3 cup orange juice
¼ teaspoon salt

Beat whites of eggs and cream of tartar until stiff.

Add yolks one at a time, beating well before the addition of each one.

Then add sugar gradually still using egg beater.

Remove egg beater; add orange rind.

Fold in flour sifted with baking powder alternately with orange juice.

Bake in moderate oven in two layer pans for 18 minutes.

Filling:

¼ cup sugar
½ cup orange juice
¼ teaspoon salt
1½ tablespoons flour

2 teaspoons grated orange rind
2 teaspoons butter
1 egg yolk

Mix all in double boiler adding yolk last, and cook until smooth and thick.

Spread between layers.

Icing:

1 unbeaten egg white
7/8 cup of granulated sugar
3 tablespoons cold water

Put in saucepan over boiling water and beat for 7 minutes. Add:

½ teaspoon flavouring
½ teaspoon baking powder

Pour over cake and sprinkle with grated orange rind.

Perfect Yellow Cake

1 cup butter or substitute
2 cups sugar
4 eggs
3 cups cake flour
4 teaspoons baking powder
1 cup milk
¼ teaspoon salt
2 teaspoons vanilla

Sift flour, add baking powder and salt. Sift three times.

Cream butter and sugar gradually, creaming mixture thoroughly.

Add eggs, one at a time, beating mixture hard after each egg is added.

Add a small amount of flour, mix well then add a little milk.

Continue in this manner until all flour and milk are used, beating batter hard after each addition.

Add flavouring.

Bake in 2 nine-inch layer pans in moderate oven (374° F), 25 to 30 minutes.

Use the following icing or any icing you prefer.

Butter Cream Icing:

1/3 cup butter
2 cups approximately icing sugar
1 teaspoon vanilla
1/8 teaspoon salt

Cream butter.

Add sifted sugar, salt and vanilla.

For variety, use lemon juice instead of vanilla and grated rind of lemon – or orange, and sprinkle coconut – or add a small mashed banana and decorate cake with slices of banana, but serve immediately as banana turns dark – unless sprinkled with lemon juice (proportion ½ lemon to a small cup of water) – or two squares of melted bitter chocolate – or black coffee to flavour. Use your own inspiration.

This makes a very large cake.

It may be baked in a sheet or in cupcake tins etc.

Pineapple Upside Down Cake

2 tablespoons butter
6 tablespoons brown sugar
1 tin sliced pineapple

Melt the butter in bottom of tin. Add sugar and spread evenly in bottom of pan.

Arrange pineapple slices over the surface with a cherry in the centre of each.

Batter:

2 tablespoons butter
5 tablespoons sugar
1 egg
1 cup of flour (sufficient to make right consistency)
2 teaspoons baking powder
½ teaspoon salt
1 teacup milk

Cream butter and sugar; add egg.

Sift dry ingredients and mix with milk. Beat well until smooth, then, pour over the slices.

Bake in moderate oven for 30 minutes.

Serve hot with cream or as a cake. Turn out, making fruit come on top.

Plain Cake

1 cup butter
1 ½ cups sugar
4 eggs
3 cups flour mixed
1 teaspoon baking powder
1 cup milk
1½ cups raisins
½ cup candied peel

Cream butter and sugar.

Add egg yolks one at a time, beat thoroughly.

Then add milk gradually and beat well.

Stir in flour and baking powder slowly.

And then add all the whites of the egg beaten stiff and lastly the raisins and peel.

Bake in a moderate oven for 30 minutes.

Raisin Cake

2 tablespoons butter
1 teacup sugar
2 eggs
2 cups flour
1 teaspoon baking powder
½ cup milk approximately
4 handfuls raisins

Cream butter and sugar.

Add well beaten eggs.

Then add raisins and mix well.

Add flour sifted with the baking powder and the milk alternately.

If mixed too wet, the raisins will sink to the bottom of the cake.

Bake in moderate oven for about 30 minutes.

Red Devil Cake

½ cup melted butter
1 cup sugar
1 egg
1½ cups flour
1 teaspoon baking powder
1 teaspoon bicarbonate soda
1 teaspoon salt
1 cup sour milk
½ cup cocoa flavouring to taste

Mix all dry ingredients.

Add the melted butter and the milk.

Then add the egg, well beaten, and flavouring to taste.

Bake in moderate oven for about 35 minutes.

Jam Sandwich Roll

2 eggs
4 tablespoons flour
3 tablespoons sugar
A pinch of baking powder

Beat well the egg yolks and sugar, adding a tablespoon of hot water to the yolks.

Add the flour and baking powder gradually, and lastly beat in the stiffly, beaten egg whites.

Pour into a well-buttered sandwich tin and bake in a moderate oven for 10 minutes.

When cooked, turn out on to a sugared (icing) paper and roll up.

When cold, unroll and cover with the following and roll up again.

Filling:

Mix icing sugar with butter and a little brandy.

Savoury filling:

Chopped ham, mixed with chopped parsley, mayonnaise and lettuce.

Scotch Cake

½ cup butter
2 cups sugar
9 eggs
3 cups flour
2 tablespoons brandy
12 drops essence of lemon
1 cup seedless raisins
½ cup candied peel

Beat the butter and sugar to a cream, then break in the eggs one by one, beating well all the time.

Next, add the brandy and essence of lemon.

Then the sifted flour, and lastly, the raisins and peel.

Put into, either one large tin or two medium sized ones, which have been well buttered.

Bake in a moderate oven for about one hour if in two tins, or longer if in one tin,

This cake will keep fresh for some weeks.

Belgian Shortbread

2 cups flour
2 teaspoons baking powder
1 cup sugar
1 cup butter (8 ozs)
1 egg
Essence
A pinch of salt

For the filling:
Jam, chopped dates, sultanas and chopped nuts

Mix butter and sugar.

Add egg, then flour and other ingredients.

Halve and roll out, and put on bottom of baking tin.

Spread with apricot jam, then chopped dates, then sultanas and chopped nuts.

Roll other half and put on top.

Bake in fairly slow oven.

Cut into squares when half cold.

Canadian Shortbread

10 tablespoons oats
7 tablespoons brown sugar
2 tablespoons flour
6 tablespoons melted butter
Almond or vanilla flavouring

Mix all ingredients together.

Pat down to about ¾ inch thick in a shallow tin, well buttered.

Bake in a hot oven for 15 to 20 minutes.

Leave it to cool slightly then cut in fingers with a knife.

Scotch Shortbread

3 cups flour
1¼ cups sifted castor sugar
½ cups slightly melted butter
10 drops almond essence
1 tablespoon ground rice (optional)

Mix together all the ingredients.

Then add sufficient milk to make into a stiff paste.

Next, roll out until an inch thick.

Bake in a moderate oven for 45 minutes.

Shortbread

2 cups butter
1 cup sugar
2 cups flour
2 tablespoons corn flour

Cut butter into small pieces and work into flour and sugar.

Roll out until an inch thick.

Bake in moderate oven for approximately 45 minutes.

Soda Cake

6 tablespoons butter
1 cup castor sugar
3 eggs well beaten
3¼ cups flour
1 small teacup boiling milk
1¼ cups sultanas
A little grated lemon rind

Beat all ingredients well together; then add:

1 small teaspoon of bicarbonate of soda

Bake from 1 to 1 ½ hours.

Sponge Cake – I

Weight of 5 eggs in sugar
Weight of 3 eggs in flour
6 eggs
Rind of 1 lemon

Put sugar and eggs into a shallow bowl; add to this the grated rind and beat for 20 minutes.

Then stir in the flour, as lightly as possible.

Put into well buttered tin and bake in a brisk oven for about 10 minutes.

Sponge Cake – II

1 tablespoon sugar
7 eggs
1 heaped tablespoon flour

Beat up the egg yolks with the sugar and flour for 10 minutes.

Add the stiffly beaten whites.

Bake in quick oven for about 10 minutes.

When cooked, turn out on damp cloth and add whipped cream and roll up quickly.

Favourite Sponge Cake

3 eggs
1 cup castor sugar
3 tablespoons boiling water
2 tablespoons potato flour
Almost 1 cup pastry flour
1 teaspoon baking powder

Break eggs into a basin and beat up with an egg beater, adding the sugar.

Then add the really boiling water and beat until light and creamy.

Put potato flour into a cup and fill the cup with pastry flour, mix well with baking powder.

Add gradually to the mixture, beating constantly.

Bake for about 8 minutes in a moderate oven.

Sultana Cake

8 dessertspoons butter
1 cup sugar
6 eggs
2 cups flour
1 ½ teaspoons baking powder
1 teaspoon ground almonds
2 teacups sultanas

Cream butter and sugar.

Switch eggs (whites separate) and add alternately with the flour.

Then mix in other ingredients.

Add in baking powder with last grains of flour.

Bake in moderate oven for 1 ½ to 1 ¾ hours.

Sunshine Cake of Yellow Maize

½ cup butter
1 cup sugar
1 egg
1½ cups white flour
1 ½ cups cornmeal
3 teaspoons baking powder
A little milk

Cream butter then add the sugar, egg and milk.

Add the dry ingredients and mix thoroughly.

Bake for one hour in a hot oven.

Swiss Roll

¾ cup sugar
4 eggs
1 cup sifted flour
2 teaspoons baking powder
¼ teaspoon grated nutmeg
A pinch of salt

Mix sugar and yolk of eggs, beat well.

Add whites of eggs beaten stiff.

Then the flour, baking powder, salt and nutmeg sifted together.

Bake from 8 to 10 minutes in a hot oven.

When baked, turn out on paper dusted with sugar.

Spread with lemon curd or jam while the cake is still hot, and roll.

Vinegar Cake – I

¾ cup butter
1 cup sugar
3 ½ cups flour
1 teaspoon bicarbonate of soda
1 tumbler milk
1 tablespoon vinegar
1 cup chopped walnuts
1 cup sultanas
½ cup raisins
¼ cup candied peel

Rub butter and flour together.

Add all the dry ingredients and mix well; in the middle.

Pour in liquids (the vinegar mixed with the bicarbonate of soda in a tumbler with half the milk).

Add rest of the milk and beat all well together.

Pour into greased tin and bake 1 ½ to 2 hours in a moderate oven.

Vinegar Cake – II

2 teacups flour
2 tablespoons butter or lard
3 or 4 tablespoons sugar
1 teacup raisins
2 tablespoons candied peel
1 teaspoon baking powder
½ mixed spice
½ teaspoon bicarbonate of soda
1 teacup milk
1 tablespoon vinegar
A pinch of salt

Sift the flour, salt, sugar, baking powder and spices into a basin, and rub in the butter with the tips of the fingers.

Add the fruit, carefully prepared, mix it in and make a well in the centre.

Put the bicarbonate of soda into a cup and mix it smoothly with the milk.

Add the vinegar, and while the mixture is still effervescing, pour it into the centre of the dry ingredients.

Mix quickly and lightly and pour at once into a greased tin.

Bake in a moderate oven until well risen, lightly browned and firm to the touch.

Walnut Cake – I

2 tablespoons butter
A small cup of sugar
4 eggs
2 cups chopped walnuts
1 tablespoon grated chocolate
Vanilla flavouring
1 cup flour
2 tablespoons baking powder
Whipped cream and some chopped walnuts for filling and topping.

Beat the butter and sugar to a cream.

Add the eggs separately.

After beating well, add the walnuts, chocolate, vanilla, the flour and baking powder.

Bake in sandwich tins.

Put whipped cream and chopped walnuts between layers and on top.

Walnut Cake – II

1 small cup butter
1 small cup sugar
3 eggs
2 cups flour
2 teaspoons baking powder
½ small cup milk
2 cups chopped nuts

Beat sugar and butter to a cream.

Add in one egg at a time and beat well.

Then add the flour and baking powder.

Lastly, add the milk and nuts.

Bake in layers or loaf.

Butter icing:

Icing sugar
Butter
1 egg white

Beat sufficient icing sugar and butter adding beaten white of egg to make the right consistency for spreading.

Walnut Surprise Cake

½ cup butter
1 ½ cups sugar
3 eggs
3 cups flour
4 teaspoon baking powder
½ teaspoon salt
1 cup milk
1 ½ teaspoons vanilla
Nut filling

Cream the shortening, adding the sugar gradually.

Next, add the beaten eggs.

Then the sifted dry ingredients, alternating with the milk, to which the flavouring has been added.

Beat well and bake in 2 greased sandwich tins for 25 minutes.

Then spread with the following nut filling:

2 cups granulated sugar
2 egg whites
½ chopped walnuts
2/3 cup hot water

Boil the sugar and water, without stirring, until syrupy.

Beat the egg whites stiff and add the syrup gradually, beating constantly.

When cool, mix in the nuts.

Strawberry Icing:

Before the cake is quite cold, cover with an icing made with strawberry juice and sufficient icing sugar to make it of the right consistency to spread.

Decorate with walnuts and strips of angelica.

Small Wedding Cake

3 cups butter
2 cups sugar
10 eggs
3 cups fine flour
2 cups sultanas or raisins
2 cups currants
1 cup candied cherries
1 cup candied peel
1½ cups sweet ground almonds
1 cup dates (optional)
1 teaspoon cinnamon
½ teaspoon nutmeg
½ teaspoon allspice
½ wine glass white wine
1½ wine glasses brandy
A pinch of salt

Soak fruit overnight in brandy.

Cream the butter, stir in sugar and beat well.

Add eggs, one at a time, beating well.

Sift half the flour with the spices and salt. Beat for 30 minutes.

Sift the remaining flour over fruit and add to the mixture with the ground almonds, the wine and the brandy.

Bake in tin, or in 2 different sized tins, with several layers of buttered paper underneath, in a fairly hot oven.

Cover the top with buttered paper.

The heat should not be too fierce, but moderate to bake the cake through.

Bake from 3 to 4 hours (less time required if 2 tins are employed).

Spread with a thick layer of the following almond paste, and cover with a thick coating of the Royal icing.

Almond Paste:

First make a syrup of:

2 tablespoons icing sugar and 1 tablespoon water

Allow to boil quickly for a few minutes, cool slightly and brush over the cake.

Then spread over the almond paste.

6 tablespoons castor sugar
6 tablespoons icing sugar
1 egg or 3 yolks
2½ cups ground almonds
1 teaspoon rose water
1 teaspoon vanilla or violet essence

Mix all well together.

Turn the paste on to a well sugared board and roll out to the size of the cake to be iced.

Spread paste over the cake, after brushing with the syrup.

When quite dry, coat with Royal icing.

Royal Icing:

4 ½ cups icing sugar
4 egg whites
A few drops of lemon juice

Sift the sugar through a hair sieve into a basin.

Break up the whites but do not beat them.

Add these to the sugar a little at a time, until all have been thoroughly mixed.

Then add the lemon juice and beat well until it is perfectly smooth and white.

Colourings may be used according to the chosen design of the cake.

Whipped Cream Cake

1 cup sugar
2 eggs
1¾ cups flour
2½ teaspoons baking powder
¼ teaspoon salt
1 cup thick cream
1 teaspoon vanilla

Whip cream until thick, add egg yolks and continue to beat until foamy.

Add sugar gradually, and the vanilla essence, and beat well.

Sift together flour, baking powder and salt and add gradually, also the stiffly beaten whites.

Bake in greased loaf pan for about 1 hour.

When cold, cover with the following chocolate butter icing.

Butter Icing:

¼ cup butter
1½ squares chocolate
1½ cups icing sugar
A little milk

Cream butter and add sugar gradually, working in well. Add the chocolate, melted in the milk, and beat well.

Icing

American Icing

3 cups granulated sugar
2 egg whites
1 small cup water

Put the sugar and water into a clean saucepan and allow the sugar to dissolve slowly.

Bring to the boil, and allow to boil 6 or 7 minutes according to the rate of boiling, timing it from the moment the sugar has dissolved, and the mixture begins to boil; do not stir.

Meanwhile, whisk the whites to a very stiff froth in a large bowl, and when the syrup is ready pour over the whites, whisking all the time.

Continue stirring until the icing cools and thickens sufficiently to coat the cake thickly, at the same time running over it smoothly - very little should run off the cake.

It should set very quickly at this point and care must be taken not to whisk too long or the icing will not run.

Any remains of this icing, may be used as a filling between sandwich cakes etc.

Chopped nuts, apricot jam or fruit juice may be mixed with it.

Never-Fail Chocolate Frosting

1 *bar sweet chocolate (7 ozs)*
2 *tablespoons butter*
1 *cup sifted icing sugar*
¼ *cup hot milk*

Melt chocolate over hot water.

Add butter and icing sugar.

Add hot milk slowly.

Beat until smooth and satiny, spread on cake.

Coffee Icing

2 cups icing sugar
1 egg yolk
A little strong coffee

Beat egg yolk well.

Pour over the hot coffee and add sugar until the right consistency to spread.

Cut the cake into layers and fill with chopped dates or with prunes that have been previously soaked in brandy.

Never-Fail Icing - Ready in 4 minutes

1 cup sugar
2 egg whites
¼ teaspoon cream of tartar
3 tablespoons water
Flavouring to taste

Place all ingredients in a double boiler over boiling water and beat constantly with an egg whisk.

Beat until the mixture leaves a hole when the beater is removed.

After removing from the fire continue beating until it is stiff enough to spread.

Nut Filling and Icing

5 tablespoons butter
3 cups icing sugar
½ cup granulated sugar
¾ cup boiling water
3 to 4 tablespoons thin cream
½ chopped nuts

Melt the granulated sugar slowly in saucepan over low flame, stirring until light golden brown.

Add boiling water slowly stirring constantly.

Boil until it reaches consistency of thick syrup.

Cool.

Cream butter.

Add icing sugar gradually.

Add cold syrup and cream slowly until right consistency to spread.

To a third of this, add the chopped nuts, and spread between layers.

With the remaining plain icing, cover the top and sides of the cake.

Sea-Breeze Frosting

2 cups sugar
2 egg whites
1 teaspoon golden syrup
1 cup approximately boiling water
1 teaspoon vanilla

Place in a saucepan over low heat the sugar, syrup and boiling water.

Stir until the mixture boils.

Then cook until it makes a thread, or when tested in cold water it forms a soft ball.

Remove from the fire and pour over the stiffly beaten egg whites.

Beat quickly until cold.

Add flavouring and continue beating until it is of the right consistency to spread.

White Icing - (hard icing)

3 cups granulated sugar
1 cup milk
1 pinch bicarbonate soda
1 teaspoon vanilla essence
A little lemon juice

Boil until a soft ball forms when tested in cold water.

Then add vanilla and lemon juice and beat until stiff.

Fillings

Delicious Chocolate Filling

This filling is ideal for pies, tart shells or cream puffs.

2/3 cup soft sugar
2 eggs or 2 egg yolks
1/3 cup sifted flour
1/8 teaspoon salt
1 bar sweet chocolate (7 ozs)
2 cups scalded milk
1 teaspoon vanilla

Melt chocolate in double boiler, or over a pan of hot water, never over direct heat.

Also scald milk over hot water.

Mix the dry ingredients and the scalded milk very slowly, and beat with an egg beater until smooth.

Put back over the hot water in pan or double boiler and cook 15 minutes, stirring constantly until the mixture thickens, and afterwards occasionally (it will look like thick white paste).

Add eggs, slightly beaten, and beat with egg beater.

Cook in double boiler 3 to 5 minutes longer. Remove from stove.

Add melted chocolate and beat with egg beater; add vanilla and cool. It will become very thick.

Fill small pastries with a tablespoon of this mixture, and a big dab of whipped cream on top.

This recipe fills about 8 to 10 little pastries or tarts.

Filling for Leftover Egg Yolks

½ cup sugar
4 egg yolks
½ cup cream
Lemon juice

Beat egg yolks until frothy.

Add the cream, sugar and enough lemon juice to make the right consistency.

Cook over hot water until it thickens.

Lemon Cheese Filling

1/2 cup butter
2 cups sugar
6 egg yolks
4 egg whites
Grated rind of 2 lemons
Juice of 3 lemons

Put into a pan and simmer gently until as thick as honey.

This quantity will make a 2 lb. jar.

Synthetic Cream

This recipe is sufficient for a two layer cake.

1 teacup castor sugar
¼ teacup water
1 egg white
1 scant cup creamed butter
2 spoonfuls of rum, bandy or strong coffee for flavouring

Make a syrup with the sugar and water.

Boil for 5 to 6 minutes without stirring – must not crystallize.

Pour over the stiffly beaten egg white and whisk briskly for a moment.

Fold in creamed butter.

Flavour with rum or brandy.

To make Mocha cream, substitute for the rum, 2 tablespoons of cold strong coffee.

Dear Reader,

We are very interested in your comments and feedback on this work. Please help us by commenting on this book. You can do so by leaving a review after reading it in your e-book reader or at the store of purchase. You can also e-mail us at the following address: *info@editorialimagen.com*

For more books, visit the following site *Editorialimagen*.com to view new titles available and take advantage of the discounts and special prices we publish each week. You can contact us directly from there if you have any questions or suggestions. We look forward to hearing from you.

More Books

A Recipe Book For Cupcakes, Biscuits And Homemade Sweets - A Selection Of British Favourites

Any time of day is the right time for something sweet. 114 recipes for delicious cupcakes, biscuits, scones, waffles, homemade bread, icings, fillings and homemade sweets. The recipes are quick and easy to prepare.

Desserts and Ice Creams - English Favourites: A selection of the best British recipes.

More than 130 desserts including boiled puddings, tarts, fruit tarts, desserts with gelatine, sauces to accompany the desserts, and ice cream.

Spanish Related Books

Las Más Fáciles Recetas de Postres Caseros

Esta selección contiene recetas prácticas que, paso a paso, enseñan a preparar los postres, marcando el tiempo que se empleará, el coste económico, las raciones y los ingredientes.

Recetas Vegetarianas Fáciles y Baratas - Más de 100 recetas vegetarianas saludables y exquisitas

Si buscabas recetas de cocina vegetariana este libro de recetas veganas es para ti. El mismo es un recetario- que contiene una selección de recetas vegetarianas saludables y fáciles de preparar en poco tiempo. Este recetario incluye más de 100 recetas para toda ocasión, y contiene una serie de platos sin carnes ni pescados, con una variedad de recetas de Verduras, Huevos, Queso, Arroz, Ensaladas.

Recetario de Tortas con sabor inglés

Si buscabas recetas de cocina británica este libro es para ti. El mismo contiene una selección de recetas de tortas con sabor inglés. Este recetario incluye 80 recetas para toda ocasión, las cuales van desde lo más sencillo hasta lo más especial, como por ejemplo, una boda.

Recetas de Pescado y Salsas con sabor inglés

Recetas populares y a la vez muy fáciles, de la cocina británica. El recetario presenta diferentes maneras de cocinar el pescado, como así también tartas de pescado y salsas para acompañar el pescado.

Recetas de Sopas con sabor inglés

La sopa es un plato saturado de proteínas y nutrientes, es muy fácil de elaborar y además, apetece a cualquier hora del día. En la dieta inglesa la sopa es muy importante.

www.ingramcontent.com/pod-product-compliance
Lightning Source LLC
LaVergne TN
LVHW011719060526
838200LV00051B/2961